THE PROPER LIMITS

OF THE

STATE'S INTERFERENCE

IN

EDUCATION.

An Address

DELIVERED ON THE 27th DECEMBER, 1860, BEFORE THE

UNITED ASSOCIATION OF SCHOOLMASTERS OF GREAT BRITAIN.

BY HARRY CHESTER, Esq.,

AN HONORARY MEMBER OF THE ASSOCIATION; A VICE-PRESIDENT OF THE SOCIETY
FOR THE ENCOURAGEMENT OF ARTS, MANUFACTURES, AND COMMERCE;
AND FORMERLY AN ASSISTANT-SECRETARY OF THE COMMITTEE
OF COUNCIL ON EDUCATION.

Published at the Request of the Association.

LONDON:
BELL AND DALDY, 186, FLEET STREET.
1861.
Price Fourpence.

THE

𝔓𝔯𝔬𝔭𝔢𝔯 𝔏𝔦𝔪𝔦𝔱𝔰 𝔬𝔣 𝔱𝔥𝔢 𝔖𝔱𝔞𝔱𝔢'𝔰 𝔍𝔫𝔱𝔢𝔯𝔣𝔢𝔯𝔢𝔫𝔠𝔢

IN

EDUCATION.

In the title of my address you will see implied an opinion that the State's intervention in the work of educating the people is at best an interference; and that there are limits beyond which it is not proper, but within which it is proper, for the State to interfere in that work.

In the half-hour allotted to me I shall not attempt to treat so great a subject completely, or even methodically. I shall merely endeavour to draw your attention to one or two of the many points which especially deserve consideration when Parliament is about to review the state of popular education, and its relations to a department of the Government. It seems to me to be of the greatest importance that, before the country is invited to take a fresh step towards the consolidation, or, it may be, towards the reduction, of the powers of the Committee of Council, the principles on which our National Education should be governed should be very carefully considered.

I am not about to criticise the proceedings of the Education Department; I have to deal with constitutional and general principles, which do not require illustration from particular "Minutes," or "Orders in Council."

We may start from a point of agreement, which is common (I hope) to all of us, that the Executive Government of the State should do for the people of this country nothing whatsoever that the people could do nearly as well for themselves.

In every Government, whether of a country, a parish, a society, or an institution, there is a natural tendency to encroach on the wills of the governed, and to subdue them to its own will, not commonly from a wish to do evil, but rather from a wish to do good, but to do it in one's own way, from a conviction of one's own superior wisdom. This tendency can only be held in check and overcome by knowledge, and a free spirit of intelligence, in the governed. This knowledge and free spirit are mainly results of education—I use the word education in its large sense, and not as merely equivalent to the word instruction; and to give to the Government of a people the control of their education is to give the advantage to the wrong side, and to deprive the governed of their best safeguard against the encroachments and abuses of their rulers. A Government ought to represent the results of the education of a well-educated people. The education of a people ought not to take its tone and character from their Government. In Prussia the education of the entire people is under the direction of the Government, a mere affair of police; and what is the consequence? There is no real liberty in Prussia. The whole body of teachers are trained in subservience to the Government, and they bring up the whole of their pupils in habits of the same subserviency.

In our own time and country, it is true that the tendency of Governments to usurp and encroach, and to endeavour to mould the popular will, is pretty well held in check, because it has been our habit to prevent the Government from improperly meddling with our affairs; but we should remember the circumstances under which this has been accomplished, and be careful lest, creating circumstances of an opposite tendency, we bring about very different results. Till a recent period, the education of those classes among us who have been educated, had been singularly independent of the political Government; and we may be sure that, if this had not been the case,—if we and our ancestors for a long period, for centuries, had lived under a Government which had held in its control the education of all classes of the people, our love of freedom and our independence would have fallen very far short of their present excellence. If Oxford and Cambridge, Eton, Westminster, Rugby, our grammar schools, and other seminaries of sound learning and manly thought, had been managed, or guided, "inspected" it is called, from time immemorial, by the Officers of State, the Lord Keeper, Mister Secretary, or even a Committee of the King's Council, do you think that our national spirit of freedom would not have suffered? that our national scholarship, intelligence, and vigour, would not have been enfeebled and stunted?

The wider education extends, the more important it is that it should be free, and "consonant with the genius of our institutions." We see education happily in course of extension among the whole community, and as it extends, it enlarges the basis of political power. If the great masses of population were for ever to be excluded from the parliamentary franchise, their being educated under the direction of the Government would be of comparatively less moment in a political point of view; but, inasmuch as happily it is quite certain that the parliamentary franchise, and political influence, will gradually descend lower and lower, it is of very great importance that the education of those masses may be in independent hands, in the guidance of the educated classes at large. The basis of a national education should be as wide and varied as possible, so as truly to represent the nation, instead of being placed in the hands of the Government of a day, which represents now one, now another, of the political parties struggling for power, and strongly tempted to use every kind of influence within reach for the advancement of their own views.

I do not pretend to define accurately all the conditions in which the State's interference in education may be proper. Let us say broadly that in education, as in everything else, the State may interfere when necessary, but its interference should be withdrawn as soon as the necessity has passed away. The normal condition of education should be freedom from the interference of the State, but that interference may properly take place under such abnormal circumstances as those of 1839. I do not in the least doubt that the creation of the Committee of Council on Education was a proper act of interference, justified because required by the abnormal necessities of the case. To save a republic a Dictator may be created. To secure elementary education, it was right to place it under the guidance of a public office. No power short of the State's executive power was then adequate to the work required; and no one who compares the state of education in Great Britain in 1839 and in 1860 can doubt that our present immense improvement could not otherwise have been reached than by the aid of the direct action of the goment. While, however, we joyfully and gratefully acknowledge the sterling good that we have derived from this source, we ought not to overlook its abnormal character. When the need of the Dictator has passed away, the dictatorship should be brought to an end; and when hereafter the need of the State's direct interference in education shall have passed away, it ought to cease to exist. There is no reason why our National and British schools should be kept, more than schools of any other kind, permanently under the control of the Government. Are we prepared to place permanently under the control, *i.e.*, nominally under the inspection, of a department of the political government, the Universities of Oxford and Cambridge, and the great public schools, grammar schools, and middle schools? If not,—and I hope and believe that we are not,—we ought steadily to keep in view the duty of preparing for the time when our National and British Schools may be released from the control of the officers of the state, and may be brought into harmony, as respects their constitution and management, with the other Educational Institutions of the country.

It must not be supposed that, when the Committee of Council was created, in 1839, the Government intended that this central body should be permanently in charge of the National Education. It was rather designed to pave the way for the establishment of a more constitutional system, in which local bodies should exercise authority over local schools, not without central supervision, and should administer local rates for education. On the 6th of March, 1856, Lord John Russell, moving his celebrated resolutions on education, said, "I do not think it was intended by those who, in 1839, commenced this system, that its plan should be such as to pervade the whole country. On the contrary, the object was rather to create models of teaching, and to exhibit such improvements in the mode of education, that the obstacles which stood in the way of a National Education might, in the process of time, be removed, and a scheme propounded for which experience may be said to presage success."

For some time after the appointment of the first Committee, attempts were repeatedly made, but without success, to procure the enactment of statutes which should constitute local authorities for the extension and improvement of education; but, in those days, when religious disunion was more potent and virulent than in these wiser days, what the Church was disposed to accept was rejected by Dissent; and what Dissent had a mind to was unpalatable to the Church. Successive administrations were discouraged by the failure of well-meant efforts at legislation for education; and, while religious parties were jangling and struggling, the work of education was constantly pushed on by the Education Department, which, consequently, grew in strength and popularity, until it has attained to such a pitch of power and authority as no one would have dreamed of conferring upon it in the days of its original establishment. The Lord President of the Council is now the Minister of Public Instruction for the Poor; and his office is a patron, a nursing father, a judge, a university to their schools.

It is not creditable to this country that so many years have elapsed without any effectual effort to establish, by authority of Parliament, a system of local self-government in education. By voluntary associations, however, something has been done to indicate some of the objects and modes of combination for the purposes of education, which are possible to religious men comprehending the limits of their own responsibilities, and not presuming to be a conscience to others.

As the grants have grown, the objections to the unconstitutional character of this Ministry of Public Instruction have ceased to make themselves heard. The one cry has been for extension, for more money, on milder conditions. Where is it all to end? It is clear that the Parliamentary grants, and the powers of the Government, acting through the Committee of Council, for the promotion of education cannot be maintained much longer within their present limits. On the one hand, the shadow of perpetually increasing charges, which have grown from £30,000 in 1839, to £798,167 in 1860, though they were intended never to exceed £100,000, has loomed large and threatening before the Chancellor of the Exchequer and the House of Commons; and the determination to reduce those charges has been so clearly indicated that their increase has been already arrested, and various retrenchments have been made. On the other hand, we have not nearly reached the limits of necessary expenditure on education. We have established an elaborate and expensive system, which was intended to educate the people, but which has taken very little effect, except in reference to little children under eleven and twelve years of age. For some time we flattered ourselves that in this system we had the means of a national education, but we have lately awakened to perceive that this notion is not only flattering but fallacious. We understand now that, in the elementary National and British school, we can do little more than to lay the mere foundations, to give the mere rudiments, of education; and that efforts, even greater and more expensive than those by which we have established our elementary schools, have still to be made for the instruction of elder children and adults before we can congratulate ourselves upon the possession of adequate means of education. The promoters of the instruction of adults, the friends of evening classes, athenæums, institutes, and people's colleges, cannot be expected much longer to endure—they do not now contentedly acquiesce in, the continuance of a system which practically debars them from any but the very scantiest participation in those national funds for education which are liberally supplied, at an enormous cost, to what we may almost call infant schools, which, important as they are, can scarcely be thought of more importance than institutions for the instruction of elder children, and of men and women. I do not in the least undervalue the school for very little children, but we reduce its utility to a minimum when we leave it without its natural necessary supplement, the provision for secondary and advanced instruction. It is of little use to sow the crop if it is not to be reaped and garnered. The greatest difficulty of elementary education is that the parents of the children of the poor, being themselves uneducated, are unable to appreciate education. Educate the parents, and they will not only acquiesce, as at present, in the education of their children, but will make any necessary sacrifice for it.

If then Parliamentary Grants are to continue to be

made for education, they must include not only the education of the children, but of the adults of the working classes. Moreover, Parliamentary Grants appear to have a natural, inevitable tendency to extend themselves upwards; and we must be prepared to see the area of their incidence constantly extended, not only from little children to young persons and adults, but also from the poor by degrees to the middle classes. The line of the Poor Law, the line of destitution, is a clear line of demarcation between classes, but above that line I believe it is not possible to draw permanently any satisfactory line of demarcation between those whom the State ought and ought not to assist in procuring education. We must remember, also, that a considerable addition has yet to be made to the existing number of little poor children at school, and that the daily increase of population adds daily to that number. Is all this mass of education to be permanently in the hands of a public office? Is Parliament likely to provide the requisite funds? If the education of adults is to be aided as effectually as that of children by the Council Office, are the Institutes to be inspected by its Inspectors of Schools?

If public money is to be granted, we know that there must be some means of testing its results. The inspection of the Committee of Council on Education is most elaborate; and, when the ages of the inspected children are considered, it must be confessed that it is unreasonably expensive. In consequence of its peculiar relations to various religious communions, the Committee employs six different species of the genus Inspector,—1st, a Clergyman, to inspect schools connected with the Church of England; 2nd, a Protestant layman, to inspect the British and other Protestant schools in England and Wales not connected with that Church; 3rd, a Roman Catholic, to inspect the Roman Catholic schools; 4th, a layman of the Church of England, to inspect the Workhouse and District Union schools; 5th, a member of the Established Church of

Scotland, to inspect the schools of that Church; and 6th, a Freechurchman, to inspect the Freechurch schools. Under these circumstances, greatly to the increase of the cost, and greatly to the diminution of the utility, of the inspection, you know that, where there are large populations, three or four different Inspectors are annually sent to the same towns. Which of these gentlemen is to inspect the education of adults? To what extent are H.M.'s Inspectors, already numbering 59, to be increased? We require a great extension of the machinery and pecuniary means of education, in order that the intellectual and physical capacities of the individuals who compose the nation may receive the best possible development and direction; but I think it neither probable nor desirable that Parliament should supply the requisite increase of funds, and entrust to a department of the Government the direction of the additional machinery.

Lord Granville, in the House of Lords, on the 13th of March, 1856, expressed himself as follows:—" I agree that the efforts of the Committee of the Privy Council may be increased with advantage; but I cannot shut my eyes to the fact that a time must come when the strain upon the central authority will be greater than it can bear, and I, for one, am of opinion that, in whatever way we do it, we must ultimately have recourse to something like local government to carry on the education of the country." " Local government" may be sneered at by the un-English doctrinaire, but will be cherished as of inestimable value by the English statesman who loves the liberty of England, and understands the foundations on which it has been reared.

I have spoken of the Committee of Council on Education as being in effect a University to Elementary Schools. If it does not actually prescribe, it at least powerfully influences, the selection of the subjects to be taught, and of the books and other appliances of teaching; tests, certificates, and rewards, and by these means shapes, the knowledge acquired; remunerates

the higher kinds of success by exhibitions which we
call Pupil-teacherships; and (in granting Certificates
to teachers) grants degrees and licences to teach.

Of all the measures adopted by the Committee of
Council, those which had for their object to teach and
train a body of superior elementary teachers, and to
attach to them the advantages of an augmented salary
and an improved position, were of the greatest urgency,
and have been of the greatest use. To supply the
want of competent schoolmasters and schoolmistresses
for elementary schools was the prime vital necessity of
education when the Committee commenced its labours;
and you yourselves are witnesses, nay, many of you
are admirable examples, of the good fruit which those
measures have borne. It would not be easy to estimate
too highly the advantages—not only to elementary
education, but—to education in general, which thus
have been gained. But we shall only deceive ourselves
if we jump to the conclusion that no evil is mixed with
this good. I need not dwell upon what I regard as a
disadvantage, viz., that the teachers on this system are
drawn too exclusively from a single class, and that
class the lowest, but I must express my fear that the
time is at hand when, if the present system be maintained without modification, the market of elementary
education will be found to be seriously overstocked
with certificated masters and mistresses; and even
now the shadow of this coming evil is cast on some of
the training schools; while, on the other hand, the
certificatees are restrained from giving their services
where they are wanted the most, and would be the
most useful, in the teaching of adults, and are confined
almost entirely to the teaching of children from three
to twelve years of age. It may be that it is a condition
inseparable from the action of a Governmental department, that it acts with a stereotypic power, tending
naturally to a too great rigidity of regulation, and
persevering in interference too far and too long. Be
this as it may be, however, the certificated teachers

have peculiar privileges as well as peculiar restrictions. They have a monopoly of the privilege of teaching with a salary derived partly from the national funds; and, though I am sure that this privilege has worked well in the past, I am not of opinion that it will work equally well always in the future. It is in effect Parliamentary protection; and, though I fear that I am about to express an unpopular sentiment, I must honestly say that it is my deliberate conviction, that the case of the teacher is no exception to the general rule of political economy, that wherever there is such protection, whether it be in relation to agriculture, shipping, manufactures, or education, though the primary result may seem to be, and may really be, very beneficial to the protected, the ultimate result must inevitably be to them a cramping and dwarfing of power, an inability to rise to perfection.

In the particular case of "protection" to which I am referring there is, moreover, a peculiarity which ought to be noticed. I have spoken of the granting of degrees, as being properly the function of a University. Now, if your degrees and licences to teach, which we call certificates, were granted by a University, the graduates would have naturally a share in its government. But this is, of course, impossible when the degrees are issued by one of the political departments of the State; and I need scarcely ask you which system is the more likely to produce a robust, masculine character, that which cannot confer, or that which naturally confers, upon its subjects a power of self-government.

We probably are all of opinion—I, certainly, for one, am very strongly of opinion—that the education of this country would suffer severely if the Committee of Council were now to be brought suddenly to an end. I believe that there remains a vast amount of useful work for that body to accomplish, but nevertheless I feel very deeply convinced that every one of its measures should be so shaped as to prepare for the time when its powers, being no longer needed, may be safely surrendered to another authority more in harmony with our constitutional traditions; and that we ourselves, instead of constantly screaming to the Government with the cry of the two daughters of the horse-leech, "Give, give," should exert ourselves in our several spheres to render education independent of the control, because independent of the aid, of the state, and to lay the foundations of the new authority which may hereafter replace the "Education Department." I conceive that the great want of popular education is a University which may do for the middle and lower classes what Oxford and Cambridge, apart from the collegiate life which is in them, but not essentially of them, have done and do for the higher classes.

Why should it be thought impossible, or very difficult, to found a new University? I have seen the foundation of the two new Universities of London and Durham—why should you not live to see the foundation of the new University of (say) South Kensington? All the elements of such an Institution exist. You have only to combine them under the authority of Parliament and under the sanction of the Crown. There are all the training Colleges ready to your hand. These might be incorporated as Colleges of the University, whose governing body, when the Board of Examiners had tested the capabilities of their students, would grant to them degrees and licences to teach, the graduates, under suitable conditions, becoming members of the Senate. The Royal Academy of Art, the Royal Academy of Music, the School of Mines, the College of Preceptors, the Schools of Science and Art, and other Institutions, *quas nunc perscribere longum est*, would naturally be included in the same incorporation; and I need scarcely point out that the system of Examinations, and the Board of Examiners, which have been established by "The Society for the Encouragement of Arts, Manufactures, and Commerce," would therein fitly find their place. You are probably aware that the Society's Examinations were held in the spring

of this year (1860), before sixty-three different Local
Boards in England, Scotland, Ireland, and Wales.
In the spring of 1861 these examinations will probably be held in a considerably greater number of
places. The vast importance of the instruction of
adults is beginning to make itself adequately felt; and
it is seen that no measures for that end are satisfactory
if they are unconnected with the means of testing,
attesting, and rewarding the results of their instruction.
Not only are new institutes, under various titles, constantly springing into existence ; all the institutes,
both old and new, are gradually but rapidly becoming
more and more educational; and, under the stimulus
supplied by the Society of Arts, they are on all sides
grouping themselves into unions, which most usefully
form inner circles within the great circle of that
Society's union. The four northern counties of England have their union. Great Yorkshire has its union,
the first that was formed. Cheshire and Lancashire
have theirs. East Lancashire and South Staffordshire
have each its own well-organised union. Bucks and
Berks have their union. The union of the three
southern counties of Hants, Wilts, and Dorset is doing
an excellent work. Sussex has a union of its own,
and I hope soon to hear of the formation of several
other similar unions. In all these associations for the
encouragement of students at Institutes and Evening
Classes, and in the Union of the Society of Arts, I find
a perception of the pressing importance of the instruction of adults, male and female, and of the necessity of
providing them with both teachers and examiners; and
I find also abundant evidence of the widely-felt want
of such influences as would be most fitly exercised not
by a Society, but by a University, of Arts, Manufactures, and Commerce, if we had one.

In order that we may have such a University at the
earliest possible period, it is not necessary to make
violent changes in the Council Office. The Union of
Institutions and Evening Classes with the Society of

Arts, and the joint action of the Central and Local
Boards of Examination, are naturally consolidating year
by year the elements of a University. The great difficulty at present is the want of teachers for adults;
and while this want is severely felt, there is a large body
of highly competent teachers who are required by official regulations to confine their services almost entirely
to the day schools which are under inspection. Now,
if these regulations were relaxed, and (supposing that
the present total of the Parliamentary Grants for education cannot be raised for a while) if a portion of the
funds devoted to those schools were to be rendered
available for the teaching of adults in Institutes and
Evening Classes, by allowing the certificated teachers
to teach therein without forfeiting the official augment-
ations of their salaries, education, both elementary and
advanced, would in every way gain, and the voluntary
associations of which I have spoken would receive im-
mediately an immense stimulus and extension. I need
scarcely say that the Society of Arts itself would accept no pecuniary assistance from the Government, and
I should think it a most mischievous boon for the institutions to accept anything that would compromise
their independence; but while the certificated teachers
retain their monopoly of official salaries, and are therefore subject to restrictions, I think that those restrictions ought so far to be relaxed as to allow the certificatees to teach in the Institutions.

I am not anxious to see a new University at once
manufactured to order by Act of Parliament, or otherwise. I wish to see the gradual and natural growth of
an independent central body, having independent local
branches, not too highly stimulated by the Government, but not interfered with nor impeded by the
Government. At present some of the regulations of
the office are a serious obstacle to the growth of
institutions for teaching adults.

I conceive that the time has arrived when all the
grants of the Committee of Council on Education

should be made on a slowly expiring scale, in order
that the promoters of schools might clearly understand
that the aid of the Government was not to be permanently given, but was intended to enable them to grow
up to independence. If an Act of Parliament were
passed enabling localities to raise by rate a limited
proportion of the funds requisite to meet grants, sub-
scriptions, and school fees, for the erection of buildings
for schools and institutions, and for their maintenance,
and the maintenance of Local Boards of Examination;
and if the Committee of Council were to publish a
minute, announcing that the grants for building, capi-
tations, and pupil teachers, after a certain (not too
early) date, would be gradually diminished till they
were absolutely extinguished, I believe that the effects
would be (first) a very great immediate increase in the
erection of schools, and (second) a perfectly safe transi-
tion from an undue dependence on the Government to
independence, and to local authority, vigorous and
fruitful of good. For the inspection of the schools,
which, as the religious bodies require different inspectors, ought, I think, to be carried on by themselves, I
wish to see substituted a system of competitive examinations, not on the limited plan of the useful " Prize
Schemes," but on the comprehensive plan established
by the Society of Arts, and explained in its Programme of Examinations for 1861.

I have not forgotten the lesson of experience that
the inspection of schools by Her Majesty's inspectors is
more efficacious than inspection by the officers of a
church or a society, but the system which I propose
would not be mere inspection by such officers; their
work would be checked, stimulated, and supplemented,
by the testing of results in annual competitive examinations.

The University, when it came into existence, might
well co-exist with the Committee of Council on Education. The two bodies would, for some years, co-
operate for a common object; and, so far as the functions

of the Government would be transferable to the independent body, the transfer would be gradual and easy.

When you, or your successors, became graduates of the University, teachers would no longer be a protected class, artificially raised, and necessarily subject to numerous restrictions; they would have before them a far wider career; they would find in their ranks men drawn from a much greater variety of social origin than at present; they would become a part, not separate, but blended with the other parts, of the great scholastic profession of the country; and they would be associated with other graduates, not teachers, but most successful students, the very *elite* of the working-class, and middle class, and not a few of the higher class, having special attainments which the University had tested and recorded. Thus circumstanced, the elementary teachers would be a more liberal body than can ever be created by a Government; and would be free from the reproach which is now sometimes directed against them, that, they are too much penetrated by a class feeling, too much given to talk and to think in the grooves of the Council office, too narrow and confined in their views.

Respecting the cost of a University, I do not think it necessary to say much. My object is to direct your attention to principles rather than to details. A very small portion of the grant now annually devoted to the building of schools would suffice to provide the requisite structure for a University apart from colleges, and a very few thousands per annum would defray the expenses of the examinations, certificates, and prizes.

On the subject of " Local Rates" I will only say that I believe that they might easily be raised for the purposes to which I propose to apply them. All the plans for local rating for education which have been rejected by Parliament, have involved in some form, directly or indirectly, the government of schools by ratepayers or their representatives, but the sustentation of Local Boards of Examiners by local rates needs to involve no such government. The Local Boards in connexion with the Society of Arts, unlike " Boards of Guardians," are composed of the friends of education, representatives of the various public Institutions and schools of the neighbourhood. The Examinations are open to all, without distinction of class or party, religious or political, and while all systems of instruction are thus encouraged, and their results are thus tested, there is no interference whatever with the internal concerns of any school or Institute.

The State, by its regulations, having somewhat interfered with and crippled the institutions for the instruction of adults, might now give a temporary impetus to them, by allowing them to engage the services of the certificated teachers. This form of aid would not lead them to rely on the State, but would help them to become independent. The greatest care should be taken to avoid interference with voluntary action.

In fine, as it appears to me, the State may interfere in education whenever and wherever it may be necessary, but only for so far and so long as necessary: and the interference should always be so directed as to make education permanently independent of the Government.

When the Universities of Oxford and Cambridge needed reform, the idea of the State's interference with them was held out, year after year, to induce them to reform themselves before Parliament actually interfered. It interfered no further than was necessary. It did nothing to compromise their permanent independence. No one proposed that they should be placed under the superintendence of a Public Office. When the grammar schools were managed too much in a spirit of religious exclusiveness, Parliament interfered; but wisely limited its interference to the laying down of a principle, and left it to the authorities of the grammar schools to carry that principle into effect. No one proposed to place the grammar schools under the superintendence of a public office. Why should the schools for the poor be differently dealt with? Because they require aid from the State? But this very question which I am raising is whether they might not be gradually rendered independent of that aid; and in this question are involved, *inter alia*, the yea and nay of a university substituted for a public office, and of graduates of that university, instead of stipendiary certificatees of the Government.

On the occasion to which I have already adverted, Lord John Russell used the following words, worthy to be held in remembrance :—"In this country, in which liberty and order have existed together, and in which they are justly prized, we ought not to be behind other nations in framing a system of National Education which shall be consonant with the genius of our institutions." With all our admiration of the results of the action of the Committee of Council on Education, can any one say that the present system is " consonant with the genius of our Institutions?" From no public office issue the degrees, orders, diplomas, and licenses, which entitle our clergy, our public and grammar schoolmasters, barristers, solicitors, physicians, surgeons, apothecaries, to practice their intellectual callings. The general rule are independent action and self-government, which make manly and free minds, justly prizing the co-existence of liberty and order in the country. We know why it was necessary, for a while, that the elementary teachers should be an exception to this rule, but, at the earliest possible period, their case ought to be brought into consonance with the genius of our institutions.

I do not desire that education should be so absolutely free that there should be no test of the sufficiency of teachers; but I contend that the test should not be permanently in the hands of the Government. The poor are bad judges of the qualifications of schoolmasters; but the poor, and the rich too, for that matter, are also bad judges of the qualifications of physicians and apothecaries. What would be thought of a proposal that the Government should grant authority to the physician and apothecary to practise their craft? They receive their authority from independent, learned bodies, constituted under the sanction of the Crown, and by the power of Parliament. Why should not the elementary teacher be tested and authorised in a similar manner? That would in truth be " consonant with the genius of our institutions."

In conclusion let me say one thing. All persons concerned in education have deep reason to feel grateful to the Committee of Council on Education. While therefore, we freely discuss, on constitutional and general grounds, the various questions which must present themselves to us, as thoughtful men, concerning the future of education and the best modes of caring for it, let us avoid even the appearance of disrespect to the Council office, and let us be perfectly loyal in all our relations to it.

NOTE. The Programme of the Examinations of the Society of Arts, for 1861, may be obtained, gratis, on application to the Secretary, Society of Arts, John-street, Adelphi, London, W.C.

W. TROUNCE, PRINTER, CURSITOR-ST., CHANCERY-LANE, LONDON.

www.ingramcontent.com/pod-product-compliance
Lightning Source LLC
Chambersburg PA
CBHW081453070426
42452CB00042B/2726